WILD WICKED WONDERFUL

TOP 10:
DISGUISES

By Virginia Loh-Hagan

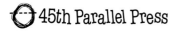

Published in the United States of America by Cherry Lake Publishing
Ann Arbor, Michigan
www.cherrylakepublishing.com

Content Adviser: Stephen Ditchkoff, Professor of Wildlife Ecology and Management, Auburn University, Alabama
Reading Adviser: Marla Conn, ReadAbility, Inc.
Book Designer: Melinda Millward

Photo Credits: ©tingfen/Thinkstock, cover, 1, 22; ©Andrew Astbury/Shutterstock Images, 5; ©Karen Kane - Alberta, Canada/ Shutterstock Images, 6; ©KMW Photography/Shutterstock Images, 6; ©Purestock /Thinkstock, 6; ©Abeselom Zerit/Shutter-stock Images, 7; ©Jeannette Katzir Photog/Shutterstock Images, 8; ©Craig Dingle /iStockphoto, 10, 11 28; ©outdoorsman/ Shutterstock Images, 12; ©MikeLane45/Thinkstock, 12; ©Erni/Shutterstock Images, 12; ©visceralimage /iStockphoto, 13; ©Rich Carey/Shutterstock Images, 14, 15, 28; ©Wong Hock weng/Shutterstock Images, 16; ©Susana_Martins/Shutterstock Images, 16; © Michael Stubblefield / Alamy Stock Photo, 17; ©Matt Jeppson/Shutterstock Images, 18; ©Mgkuijpers /Dreams-time.com, 18; ©Jason Ondreicka /Dreamstime.com, 18; ©Coy St. Clair /iStockphoto, 19; ©ChinKC/Shutterstock Images, 20; ©RidvanArda/Shutterstock Images, 21; ©Woravit Vijitpanya /Dreamstime.com, 22; ©Alberto Nieves/Shutterstock Images, 22; ©Lehakok /Dreamstime.com, 23; ©Sean Pavone/Shutterstock Images, 24; ©Fuse/Thinkstock, 26; © Jim Brandenburg/Minden Pictures/Corbis, 27; ©Ethan Daniels/Shutterstock Images, 28; ©Richard Whitcombe/Shutterstock Images, 28; ©NaturePhoto/ Shutterstock Images, 29; ©Aquanaut4 /Dreamstime.com, 30; ©Ryan M. Bolton/Shutterstock Images, 31

Graphic Element Credits: © tukkki/Shutterstock Images, back cover, front cover, multiple interior pages; © paprika/Shutterstock Images, back cover, front cover, multiple interior pages; © Silhouette Lover/Shutterstock Images, multiple interior pages

45th Parallel Press is an imprint of Cherry Lake Publishing.

Library of Congress Cataloging-in-Publication Data

Names: Loh-Hagan, Virginia, author.
    Title: Top 10 : disguises / by Virginia Loh-Hagan.
Other titles: Top ten : disguises | Disguises
Description: Ann Arbor, Michigan : Cherry Lake Publishing, [2016] | Series: Wild wicked wonderful
Identifiers: LCCN 2015026849| ISBN 9781634705028 (hardcover) | ISBN 9781634706223 (pbk.) |
ISBN 9781634705622 (pdf) | ISBN 9781634706827 (ebook)
Subjects: LCSH: Animals—Color—Juvenile literature. | Camouflage (Biology)—Juvenile literature. |
Animals—Miscellanea—Juvenile literature.
Classification: LCC QL767 .L67 2016 | DDC 591.47/2–dc23
LC record available at http://lccn.loc.gov/2015026849

Printed in the United States of America
Corporate Graphics

3 7777 13420 1375

About the Author

Dr. Virginia Loh-Hagan is an author, university professor, former classroom teacher, and curriculum designer. She's not good at disguises. Her loud laugh gives her away. She lives in San Diego with her very tall husband and very naughty dogs. To learn more about her, visit www.virginialoh.com.

TABLE OF CONTENTS

INTRODUCTION

Animals change colors. They change shapes. They blend in. They act like something else. They **disguise** themselves. They change how they look.

They mislead **prey**. Prey are animals that are hunted for food. They mislead **predators**. Predators are hunters. Animals are experts at **deception**. Deception is tricking others. They do this for different reasons. They're protecting themselves. They don't want to become food. They're hunting. They want to get food. They want to mate. They want to **survive**. They want to live.

Some animals have extreme disguises. Their disguises are bigger. Their disguises are better. They have the most exciting disguises in the animal world!

Animals disguise themselves in different ways.

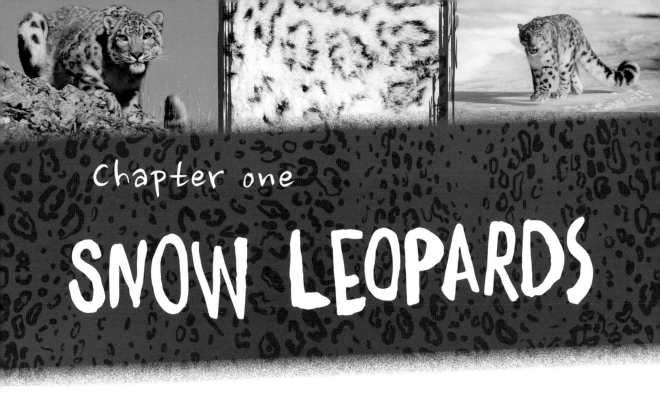

Chapter one

SNOW LEOPARDS

Snow leopards live in the Himalayan Mountains. These are the highest mountains in the world. They're in Asia.

Snow leopards love the mountain life. They can be found at 14,000 feet (4,267 meters) above sea level. They're the highest-living cats. They are made for living in the mountains. They have thick coats. They have furry tails and paws. Their paws work like snowshoes. They use their tails as scarves.

Their thick fur is white, yellow, or gray. They have ringed spots of black on brown. They **camouflage**. They hide.

Snow leopards are the top predators in the Himalayas.

They blend into their surroundings. They pretend to be rocks. Their spots blend in with the rocky background. Their light fur blends in with the snow.

Snow leopards are endangered.

It's better to have spots than to be one color. Mountains are many colors. Snow leopards' spots help them. They blend in better.

They can kill animals that are three times bigger. They mainly eat mountain sheep. These sheep can climb mountains. Snow leopards have to be smart. They **stalk** their prey. They follow them. They hide among the rocks. They wait for prey to come. Then they attack. They have powerful legs. They can leap up very high. They can jump very far.

Snow leopards want to be invisible. Having a good disguise helps them survive.

HUMANS DO WHAT?!?

Tom Leppard is also known as Leopard Man. (His real name is Tom Woodbridge.) He lives in Scotland. He had a world record. He was the world's most tattooed man. He tattooed his skin. He made himself look like a leopard. He even lived like a leopard. He lived in a small hut. He lived in a remote area. He was far away from town. He didn't have electricity. His floor was the dirt ground. His roof was a metal sheet. His bed was foam board. He cooked on a small stove. He said, "I have no interest in a TV or a radio. Nor do I want a telephone. … I'm not really that interested in what else is going on outside."

Chapter two
LYREBiRDS

Lyrebirds live in rainforests. They live in Australia. They have strong voice muscles. They can disguise their voices.

They sing all year. They sing the most from June to August. They sing for four hours per day. Male lyrebirds can copy more than 20 different birdcalls. They also copy non-bird sounds. Examples include a camera, car alarm, and chainsaw. They can sound like humans. Females also make sounds. But they're not as skilled as males. Young birds take about a year to learn sounds.

Male lyrebirds have a beautiful tail. This is used to attract mates as well.

Males do this to attract mates. The best singer gets the most females. Their songs combine their own songs and other noises.

Chapter three

ARCTIC FOXES

Arctic foxes live in the Arctic. They have white fur. This is how they stay alive. They camouflage. They blend in with snow. They hide. They hunt. They avoid predators.

They go close to polar bears. They eat the polar bears' leftovers. But they don't go too close. They don't want the polar bears to eat them.

Arctic foxes **molt**. They shed their fur. They get new fur coats. They change when the snow melts. They lose their white coats. They get their summer coats. The summer coats have different colors. They still camouflage. They change with the seasons.

Arctic foxes turn white in the winter.

chapter four
SEA SNAKES

Sea snakes mostly live in the Pacific islands. They're more than 4 feet (122 centimeters) long. They're as thick as a man's thumb. Most have black-and-white stripes. Their tails are like paddles. They weave through the water. This creates an **optical illusion**. They trick the eyes.

It looks like they're moving the other way. Their heads and tails are black. Predators can't tell what way they're going. They can't tell their heads from their tails. They think they're attacking from behind. Sea snakes fake out predators. This gives the snakes time. They can swim away. Or they can fight.

There are very few animals in the sea brave enough to take on a sea snake.

Sea snakes are related to cobras. Their teeth have poison. The poison can kill a man in six to 12 hours.

chapter five
SPIDER CRABS

Spider crabs live on the seafloor. They're known as "camouflage crabs." They're bumpy. They blend into the rocky floor.

They have **pincers**. These are crab claws. Their pincers are narrow. They're long. They wave them over their heads. This warns off predators.

They're slower and weaker than other crabs. They create disguises. They hide. They use their pincers. They trim plant pieces. They chew them. They stick the chewed ends to their bodies. They have tiny hairs on their legs and back.

Spider crabs range in size. Adult males are larger than females.

The hairs are like hooks. Spider crabs stick the plants to their hairs. They create their own cover. They hide their movements. They molt to grow. They change shells. They change for their surroundings.

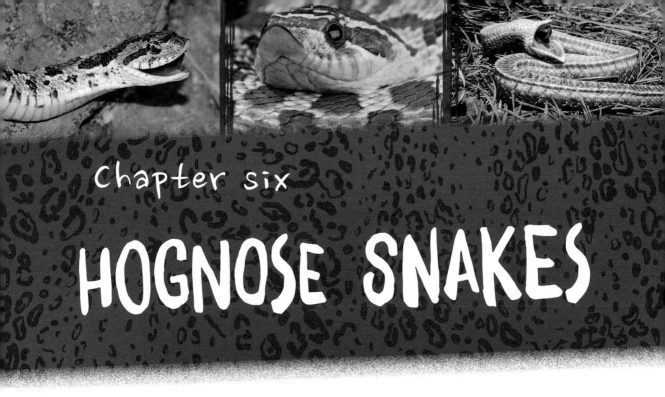

Chapter six

HOGNOSE SNAKES

Hognose snakes are common in the United States. They have **upturned** noses. Their noses point up. They dig in sandy dirt. They sweep. They go side to side. They dig up lizard eggs to eat. They're not poisonous. So they need a way to protect themselves.

The snakes act tough. They flatten their necks. They raise their heads. They look like cobras. They hiss. Sometimes, they pretend to strike.

They act dead. They roll onto their backs. They even smell dead. They give off bad smells. They poop. They let their

Hognose snake bites are rare.

tongues hang out. Predators think they're dead.

They hide. They're shy snakes. They tunnel down into leaves and sand.

19

Chapter seven

CATERPILLARS

Caterpillars look like worms. They cast off their skins. They do this at least four times. Each molt gives them more room to grow. Their colors match their surroundings.

Caterpillars use disguise to survive. Some caterpillars disguise themselves as bird **droppings**. Droppings are poop. Caterpillars don't want to look like food. Snakehead caterpillars live in South America. They disguise themselves as snakes. Their feelers flicker in and out. They look like forked tongues.

Caterpillars change their bodies. They're babies. They

change into **cocoons**. A cocoon is a silky case. Some cocoons look like leaves. Then they become butterflies or moths.

chapter eight

SEA DRAGONS

Sea dragons live in Australia. They're related to sea horses. They have long, thin **snouts**. Snouts are noses and mouths. They look like pipes. Their bodies are slender. They're covered in bony rings. They have thin tails.

They have small, clear fins. The fins move them. They glide. Their snouts are like vacuums. They suck in animals. That's how they eat.

There are two types. Leafies have brown and yellow bodies. Most of their limbs are green. They look like leaves. Weedies are not as showy. They're red. They have yellow

The male sea dragon carries the eggs that will become babies.

spots. They look like weeds.

Sea dragons face many dangers. They're slow swimmers. They can't escape from predators. They need disguises.

Sea dragons can stay in one place for up to 68 hours.

Sea dragons live among seaweed. They usually float with the plants. Their bodies are designed for deception. They camouflage. Their limbs look like leaves. They have bumps on their skin. They look like seaweed. When they swim, they look like floating seaweed. They fool many animals.

Sometimes, they can change color. They blend in. This ability depends on what they eat.

Sea dragons have an additional trick. Males carry the babies. Their tails become red. They become swollen. This lets females know they're ready. Females put eggs under their tails.

DID YOU KNOW...?

- Lyrebirds aren't the only voice mimics. Michael Winslow is known as the "Man of 10,000 Sound Effects." He uses his voice. He makes all kinds of sounds.

- Humans also disguise themselves. Spies wear many disguises. They pretend to be someone else. A New York Police Department squad wore disguises. They did this in the 1950s. The men dressed like women. They tricked about five criminals each day.

- The banded snake eel is a fish disguised as a snake. It looks and moves like a snake. Predators don't mess with snakes.

- Divers caught sea dragons. They wanted them as pets. This practice reduced their numbers. The Australian government banned the taking of sea dragons.

- Walking sticks lose limbs. They can grow new ones. Some walking sticks squirt liquid at predators. They blind predators.

- Some octopuses can use tools. They find coconut shells. They play with them. They use the shells as shelter.

Chapter nine

WALKING STICKS

Walking sticks are bugs. Their tails look like twigs. Their legs look like leaves or sticks.

They're **nocturnal**. They're active at night. During the day, they're still. They're very still. They look like branches. They sit on bark. They don't move. They copy their surroundings. They're green or brown. This protects them. They don't want to be eaten by birds.

They pretend to be dead. They'll shed limbs. Some release bad-smelling liquid. They do anything to escape predators.

Giant walking sticks can be over 21 inches (53 cm). They're one of the world's longest insects.

Baby walking sticks disguise themselves as ants. They copy how ants move. They copy how ants look. Ants are known for attacking other bugs.

chapter ten
OCTOPUSES

Octopuses live at the bottom of the sea. They have two eyes. They have four pairs of arms. They don't have bones. They can squeeze through tight places.

They use camouflage. They hide. They can change shape, color, and skin **texture**. Texture is the feel of something. They use skin muscles to change texture. This makes their disguise more real. They can change in less than a second.

They have many tiny skin **pigment** cells. Pigment is color. They make cells bigger. They make cells smaller. This is how they change colors. They match their surroundings.

Octopuses have many disguises.

Octopuses can change to look like seaweed. They can look like rocks.

Mimic octopuses are smaller. They're more flexible.

Mimic octopuses pretend to be other animals. They copy shapes. They copy movements. They copy speed. They're the only sea animals that can do this. They pretend to be more dangerous animals. They pretend to be crabs. They pretend to be lionfish. They pretend to be sea snakes.

To be sea snakes, they hide in a hole. They stick out two of their legs. The legs stick out in opposite directions. Predators see a long thin object. They see white-and-black bands. They go away.

They copy to protect themselves. But they also copy to hunt.

WHEN ANIMALS ATTACK!

Alligator snapping turtles live in the southern United States. They're the largest freshwater turtles. They can grow up to 300 pounds (136 kilograms). They have powerful jaws. They have sharp claws. They have a special hunting move. They lie still in the water. They disguise themselves as rocks. They open their jaws. Their tongues look like worms. They trick small fish, frogs, and other turtles. When prey enter their mouths, they snap their jaws shut. They instantly kill their prey. Their jaws can snap through bone. There was an attack reported in southern Germany. They think an alligator snapping turtle bit an eight-year-old boy's ankle. They're searching for the turtle. They're afraid of another attack. These turtles should not be in Germany. An official said, "The turtle is so dangerous. We have to find it. Otherwise it could get to another lake." The city calls the turtle Lotti.

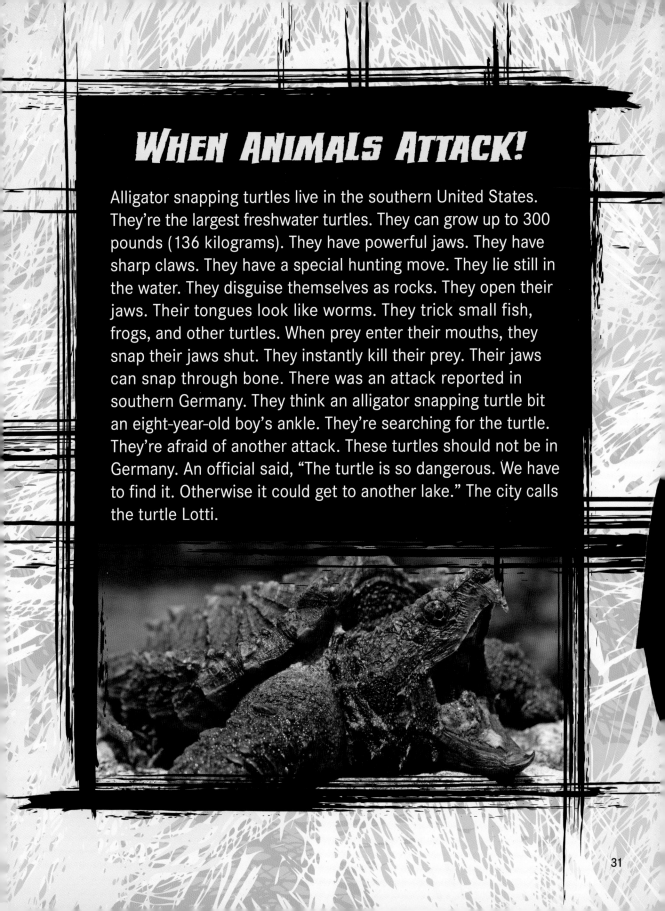

CONSIDER THIS!

TAKE A POSITION! Animal disguises help prey. They help predators. Do you think disguises benefit prey or predators more? Argue your point with reasons and evidence.

SAY WHAT? Explain different types of ways that animals disguise themselves.

THINK ABOUT IT! How do humans use disguises? In what ways are we similar to the animals featured in this book?

LEARN MORE!
* Ryan, Emma. *Animal Disguises*. New York: Scholastic, 2011.
* Weber, Belinda. *Animal Disguises*. Boston: Kingfisher, 2004.

GLOSSARY

camouflage (KAM-uh-flahzh) to blend into the surroundings

cocoons (kuh-KOONZ) silky cases for caterpillars

deception (di-SEP-shuhn) the act of misleading

disguise (dis-GIZE) something that changes appearance

droppings (DRAHP-ingz) poop

mimic (MIM-ik) copy

molt (MOHLT) to change by shedding

nocturnal (nahk-TUR-nuhl) active at night

optical illusion (AHP-ti-kuhl ih-LOO-zhuhn) something visual that tricks the eyes

pigment (PIG-muhnt) color

pincers (PIN-surz) crab claws

predators (PRED-uh-turz) hunters

prey (PRAY) animals that are hunted for food

snouts (SNOUTS) nose and mouth areas

stalk (STAWK) to follow

survive (sur-VIVE) to live

texture (TEKS-chur) the feel of something

upturned (UHP-turnd) pointing upward

INDEX